D1283802

Zora Neale Hurston

As a writer and a cultural anthropologist, Zora Neale Hurston was both a collector and a teller of stories about black life in the American Deep South.

JUNIOR ▪ WORLD ▪ BIOGRAPHIES

Zora Neale Hurston

ROZ CALVERT

CHELSEA JUNIORS 🌿

a division of CHELSEA HOUSE PUBLISHERS

Chelsea House Publishers

EDITOR-IN-CHIEF   Richard S. Papale
MANAGING EDITOR   Karyn Gullen Browne
COPY CHIEF   Philip Koslow
PICTURE EDITOR   Adrian G. Allen
ART DIRECTOR   Nora Wertz
MANUFACTURING DIRECTOR   Gerald Levine
SYSTEMS MANAGER   Lindsey Ottman
PRODUCTION COORDINATOR   Marie Claire Cebrián-Ume

JUNIOR WORLD BIOGRAPHIES

SENIOR EDITOR   Kathy Kuhtz

Staff for ZORA NEALE HURSTON

ASSOCIATE EDITOR   Terrance Dolan
COPY EDITOR   David Carter
EDITORIAL ASSISTANT   Robert Kimball Green
PICTURE RESEARCHERS   Wendy P. Wills, Michele Brisson
SENIOR DESIGNER   Marjorie Zaum
COVER ILLUSTRATION   Janet Hamlin

Copyright © 1993 by Chelsea House Publishers, a division of
Main Line Book Co. All rights reserved. Printed and bound
in the United States of America.

First printing

1 3 5 7 9 8 6 4 2

Library of Congress Cataloging-in-Publication Data
Calvert, Roz.
   Zora Neale Hurston/Roz Calvert.
     p. cm.—(Junior world biographies)
   Includes bibliographical references and index.
Summary: A biography of the versatile and prolific Afro-American writer,
well-known for her novels and collections of black folklore.
ISBN 0-7910-1766-4
ISBN 0-7910-1962-4 (pbk.)
1. Hurston, Zora Neale—Biography—Juvenile literature. 2. Novelists,
American—20th century—Biography—Juvenile literature. 3. Folklorists—
United States—Biography—Juvenile literature. 4. Afro-Americans—Intel-
lectual life—Juvenile literature. [1. Hurston, Zora Neale. 2. Authors,
American. 3. Afro-Americans—Biography.] I. Title. II. Series.
PS3515.U789Z46 1992   91-42231
813'.52—dc20   CIP
[B]   AC

Contents

Born in the all-black township of Eatonville, Florida, in 1891, Zora Neale Hurston would eventually leave the sleepy village behind to become the worldly, well-known writer and traveler pictured here.

1

Talking Birds
and Magic Lakes

At eight o'clock in the morning on October 16, 1933, Zora Neale Hurston's landlady came to Zora's house and told her to get out. Zora owed $18 for three months' rent. Zora promised she would have all the rent money by evening. She had a new job, and she would be getting paid that day. But the landlady said that she did not believe Zora would ever have enough money to pay the rent she owed.

Zora had been living in the tiny, one-room house in the town of Sanford, Florida, for three months. She had come to Sanford to write her first novel, *Jonah's Gourd Vine*. Writing a novel was a full-time job. Zora could not work at another job at the same time, so she had no money to pay the rent. Her friends and relatives helped her out as much as they could. Every week, Zora's cousin Willie Lee bought groceries for her. When the book was finished, Zora asked a friend to type the manuscript. She asked another friend for the money to mail it to publisher Bertram Lippincott in New York. Finally, the manuscript was in the mail, and Zora went out to find a job.

The day Zora was kicked out, she packed up her things and moved them to her Uncle Isaiah's house. Then, with a heavy heart, she went to work at the job she had found. That afternoon, a messenger from the Western Union telegraph office brought Zora a telegram. Zora was too busy to read it, so she put it in her dress pocket. At the end of the day, Zora collected her pay. She needed new shoes, so she went to the shoe store to buy a pair.

While she was trying on shoes, Zora remembered the telegram. She took it out and read it. "I never expect to have a greater thrill than that wire gave me," Zora remembered years later. The telegram was from Bertram Lippincott. It said that Zora's novel would be published. Zora was offered a $200 advance payment. Zora was so excited that she "tore out of that place with one old shoe and one new one on and ran to the Western Union office. Lippincott had asked for an answer by wire and they got it!"

Zora's life had changed dramatically between sunrise and sunset that day. In the morning, she was someone struggling to pay her rent. By evening, she was a successful author. But Zora was used to ups and downs. Her life had been full of them to that point, and it would continue to be, because Zora Neale Hurston was someone who took chances. She was full of curiosity and courage.

When Zora was a child, her mother had often told her to "jump at the sun." By that she meant that Zora should set the highest goals for herself and not let anything hold her back. Zora had followed her mother's advice. "We might not land on the sun," she remarked, "but at least we'd get off the ground." And on that October day in 1933, Zora got off the ground. She was on her way to becoming one of the most important black American women writers of the 20th century.

Zora Neale Hurston was born in Eatonville, Florida, in 1891. Eatonville was a very unusual town. It was the first all-black community in the United States to win the right to govern itself. Zora's parents, Lucy and John Hurston, were sharecroppers in the cotton fields of Alabama when they first heard rumors about Eatonville.

Sharecroppers—usually blacks or other poor people—tended fields that were owned by white farmers. Sharecroppers were allowed to keep a portion of the crops they grew in payment for farming the land. If the harvest was poor, the owner would still expect his crops first, and the sharecropper might be left with little or nothing. Sharecroppers like the Hurstons led a tough life. They worked long, hard hours in the fields every day, but they could never get ahead.

When John and Lucy Hurston heard about the new town in Florida, they were curious. It was said that Eatonville would be a town for black people. Blacks would run the town themselves. They would build farms and businesses of their own. And they would not have to live with the *racism* they faced in white communities. Eatonville would be a place where black families and black culture could thrive. It almost sounded like a paradise. The Hurstons quit sharecropping and moved to Florida.

By the time Zora was born, her parents were farming five acres of their own in Eatonville and had built an eight-room house. John Hurston was a well-respected citizen of the town. He served three terms as mayor and was a preacher in the Baptist church. Life was good in Eatonville.

Black sharecroppers tend to their ox teams near Tallahasee, Florida. Hurston's parents left behind the hard sharecroppers' life when they came to Eatonville in the late 19th century. In Eatonville, John Hurston, Zora's father, bought some land and built a house.

13

Although Zora had seven brothers and sisters, they never went hungry. The family raised chickens and hogs, and there was good fishing in the nearby lake. The Hurstons had a huge garden and many fruit trees on their land. There were always plenty of oranges, tangerines, grapefruits, and guavas.

Lucy Hurston taught all her children to read before they went to school. Zora especially loved to read. At home, she would read her mother's Bible. She was thrilled by the exciting stories about such figures as David and Goliath, and Moses. In school, she read as many books as she could. Once, when some white visitors came to her school, Zora was asked by the teacher to read aloud for them. The two women liked the way Zora read so much that they sent her a big box of books as a gift. The box was full of wonderful books, and Zora read them all. Her favorites were the books of Greek, Roman, and *Norse mythology*. She loved to read about the great doings of the Norse gods such as

Thor and Odin and the Greek heroes such as Hercules.

The myths that Zora read seemed familiar to her. They reminded her of stories she had been hearing all her life in Eatonville. People were always gathered on the porch of the village store, telling stories, singing, and gossiping. "Joe Clarke's store was the heart and spring of the town," Zora recalled. "For me, the store porch was the most interesting place that I could think of." There, on the porch of the general store, Zora heard the myths of black culture in the American South. They were fantastic, funny stories, full of

Eatonville's Hungerford School, which Hurston attended as a child. The young Hurston loved school, and she soon proved to be a gifted reader and writer. Those talents would serve her well in later years.

magical events, talking animals, and other strange characters. Sometimes they were about God and the Devil. And like most myths, the stories often explained things about life, death, and the way of the world.

Zora treasured these stories, which are called *folktales* or *folklore*. Whenever her mother sent her to the store, she hung around that porch as long as she could. She listened with delight to the stories and songs and the colorful language of her neighbors. She learned to become a storyteller herself. "I picked up glints and gleams out of what I heard and stored it away to turn it to my own uses," she remembered later. Zora began to make up her own stories, which she would tell to her mother. Lucy Hurston would smile at her daughter's wild imagination.

Zora told stories about talking lakes and magic birds. She made a doll out of an ear of corn and named her Miss Corn-Shuck. Then she created a boyfriend for Miss Corn-Shuck out of a bar of soap and called him Mr. Sweet Smell. She made another character called Reverend Door-Knob. Zora would spend hours making up stories about these characters.

Although Zora loved Eatonville, she was also curious about life outside the village. "I used to climb to the top of one of the huge chinaberry trees which guarded the front of our gate and look out over the world," she recalled. "The most interesting thing that I saw was the horizon." As she grew older, the books she read added to her curiosity about the world.

Zora was a late walker as a baby. She did not walk until one day when her mother went to the spring to wash some greens for dinner. Lucy left nine-month-old Zora sitting on the kitchen floor with a piece of corn bread to chew on. A big sow from the barnyard came to the door. The fully grown female pig wanted Zora's bread and came into the kitchen to get it. Little Zora decided that it was time to start walking.

Zora's long career as a wanderer had begun. "Once I found the use of my feet," Zora recalled,

Southerners swap jokes
and stories on the porch
of a general store in
North Carolina. The
porch of the general
store in Eatonville was
one of young Hurston's
favorite places, where she
loved to listen to stories
and songs about life in
the South.

"they took to wandering. I always wanted to go. I would wander off in the woods all alone, following some inside urge to go places. This alarmed my mother a great deal. She used to say that she believed a woman who was an enemy of hers had sprinkled 'travel dust' around the doorstep the day I was born."

Zora spent a lot of time wandering in the woods, where she listened to the wind, made up stories, and wondered what her future would bring. One day, she stopped to rest in the shade and fell into a strange sleep. Twelve scenes flashed before her eyes. Zora felt that these visions revealed her future. "I knew my fate," she said. "I knew I would be an orphan and homeless. I knew that while I was still helpless, the comforting circle of my family would be broken, and that I would have to wander cold and friendless." But the visions also showed Zora that she would pass through the hard times, and that better times would follow.

Afterwards, Zora always felt that her

childhood had ended on that dreamy day. And before long, the visions she had seen began to come true. When Zora was 13, her mother died. Lucy Hurston had been the heart and backbone of the family. Zora's father was not as strong. After Lucy died, the Hurston family began to unravel. Two weeks after her mother's funeral, Zora was sent away to school in Jacksonville, Florida.

Zora rode in the wagon with her brother Dick to catch the train to Jacksonville. All her belongings were packed in "a little, humped-up, shabby-backed trunk." Zora's wanderings had truly begun. Ahead of her were many adventures, hard times, and good times as well. She was eager to finally see what lay over the horizon, but she was sad about leaving Eatonville. She felt that she would never again be "a real part of the town." But she would learn that the town would always be a part of her.

Zora Neale Hurston (center) poses with two friends at Howard University in 1919. Although she was forced to leave home and give up school while still a teenager, Hurston never let go of her dream of attending college.

2

Travel Dust

When Zora Hurston arrived in Jacksonville in 1904, she found that it was a different world from Eatonville. Unlike her quiet, sleepy hometown, Jacksonville was a big, busy city. And unlike Eatonville, both blacks and whites lived in Jacksonville. But there was *segregation* in Jacksonville. This meant that blacks and whites were kept apart by laws known as *Jim Crow laws*. Blacks could not use the same restrooms or drinking fountains as whites. Blacks were not allowed to sit on the same park benches as whites. They could not go to the same schools or restaurants or theaters. Practically every aspect of day-to-day life was affected by segregation. Blacks were always reminded that they did not have the same rights and privileges as whites.

Zora now had to face racism every day, something she had never encountered in Eatonville. There, she had been Zora Hurston, the daughter of a respected family. But in Jacksonville, things were different. "Jacksonville made me know that I was a little colored girl," Zora wrote in her autobiography. She felt the sting of this racism for the first time and was puzzled by it. "These white people have funny ways," Zora remembered thinking at the time.

Zora was one of the youngest girls at the school she attended in Jacksonville. Because of her lively nature, she quickly became a well-known personality at school. The older girls thought she was a bother because she was always listening in on their private talks. The teachers thought Zora was sassy because she always had something to say, even when she was not asked. This got Zora into trouble sometimes. Teachers, Zora said, "hated backtalk worse than barbed-wire pie."

Although she occasionally got in trouble, Zora liked school and was an eager student. Her education was going along well enough until her father stopped sending money to pay for her school bills. Zora had to start doing work at the school to pay her own way. Every Saturday, she scrubbed down the stairs of the school, and after classes she cleaned up the pantry. It was hard work but Zora faced it. She finished the school year and even won a spelling bee for her school. She was given an *atlas* of the world and a Bible as prizes.

Once school let out for the summer, Zora waited for her father to come and take her home. She waited and waited. Weeks went by, but John Hurston did not come. Zora became depressed and afraid. She seemed to be losing her family, just as the visions in her dreams had told her.

Back in Eatonville, there was a new woman in John Hurston's life. Zora's father had remar-

John Hurston and his second wife in a 1906 photograph.
The arrival of John Hurston's new wife after the death
of Lucy Hurston left little room in the house for Zora,
who was soon forced to set out on her own.

ried. But his new wife did not want to share him and his house with Zora and her sisters and brothers. She did not want Zora to come home again. John Hurston went along with his new wife's wishes. He wrote a letter to the principal of Zora's school, asking if the school would adopt Zora. The principal called Zora to her office and told her about the letter. Zora felt lonely and unwanted, like an orphan. The school could not adopt Zora, so the principal gave her money to go back home.

Zora traveled by riverboat down the St. Johns River to Eatonville. She enjoyed the big riverboat. It had shiny brass railings and red carpets. At night, big lights were turned on. Zora stood on deck most of the time. She was glad to see the lush Florida countryside again. Spanish moss hung from the trees, and there were miles of blooming purple hyacinths. She watched the alligators, colorful water birds, and giant catfish in the water. Back in Eatonville, Zora was happy to be home, but things had changed. There were a lot of bad feelings in the house that had once been her home. John Hurston's young wife disliked his children and fought with them. The four older children soon left to make their own way in the world. The others, including Zora, were sent off to live with friends and relatives.

For the next five years Zora lived like a nomad. She would stay at the home of a friend or a relative for a while and then move on to a different place. Sometimes she would stay in one place long enough to attend school, but most of the people she lived with could not afford to pay for her education. These were hard years for Zora. She was miserable. "I wanted family love and peace and a resting place," she wrote. "I wanted books and school."

Zora began to look for jobs so that she could support herself and not depend on others. It was hard for her to find work because she was so young and inexperienced. Eventually, she found work as a maid. When that job ended, she found another as a maid, and then another and another.

After her mother's death and her own departure from Eatonville, Hurston became a wanderer with no true home of her own.

None of these jobs lasted for long. Zora was discouraged and frustrated. She did not want to be a maid for the rest of her life. "I was doing none of the things I wanted to do," she wrote.

Then Zora learned about a job that sounded very interesting. A friend told her that the leading singer in an *operetta* company needed a maid. If Zora got the job it would mean traveling around with the company as they went from town to town putting on shows. Zora decided to apply for the job. For the interview, Zora's friend bought her a new dress and lent her a hat. Zora shined her shoes, put on her new dress and hat, and went to the local theater to ask about the job.

Zora knocked on the dressing room door. When the singer answered, Zora told her that she had come to work for her. The singer looked at Zora and asked her how old she was. Zora lied, telling the singer that she was older than she really was. The singer, whom Zora would always call Miss M., suspected that Zora was lying. But she also liked Zora immediately. She offered Zora the job. The pay was $10 a week, a lot of money to Zora. A week later, Zora left town with the operetta company.

Zora promptly fell in love with theater life. "Everything was pleasing and exciting," she wrote. Zora traveled with the operetta company for a year and a half. She was the only black person in the company. The others teased Zora because of the way she spoke and because there were a lot of things she did not yet know about life. But the teasing was in fun, and Zora did not mind it much. Everyone in the company liked her, and she loved the attention she was receiving. It made her begin to feel "cocky as a sparrow on Fifth Avenue." Zora wrote a gossip column about the company and put it up on the bulletin board. Her column made a big hit with the company.

After 18 months, the job with the operetta company came to an end. Living with the creative show people was a learning experience for Zora. It was now time to set out on her own again. What Zora did for the next five years is a mystery. Some people think she may have been secretly married. Zora herself never revealed how she spent those years. In 1917 she turned up in Baltimore, Maryland. Now 26 years old, she was still determined to complete her education. Zora succeeded in getting a job as a waitress and began taking classes at night.

After a few months of night school, Zora applied to Morgan Academy, a high school in Baltimore. She did well on the entrance exam and was placed in the junior class at the academy. The dean of the school helped Zora get a job as a live-in companion for a sick woman. The woman's home had a large library, and Zora tried to read as many of the books as she could. In the meantime, she was becoming a popular and successful student at the academy.

Most of the students at Morgan were from well-to-do families. Zora was so poor she had only one dress to wear to school. Jokingly, her friends would ask Zora what she planned on wearing to school the next day. Zora took the joke well and would describe some gorgeous outfit. But if Zora had somewhere special to go, her girlfriends would lend her some nice clothes. These were happy, satisfying years for Zora. After her years of wandering and doubt, her dream of getting an education was finally coming true.

Zora graduated from Morgan in 1918. She began thinking about college. Howard University in nearby Washington, D.C., was one of the best black universities in the country. It was expensive and hard to be admitted to. But Zora, remembering her mother's advice to "jump at the sun," was determined to attend Howard. She moved in with friends in Washington, found a job to pay for tuition, and applied for admission to Howard. In the fall of 1919, she proudly entered Howard University as a freshman.

Being at Howard was a thrill for Zora. "I shall never forget my first college assembly, sitting there in the chapel of that great university," she wrote. Zora was so proud that she made a promise in her heart to the university. "You have taken me in," she said to the college. "I am a tiny bit of your greatness. I swear to you that I shall never make you ashamed of me."

Zora's college years were busy and exciting. When she was not attending class or studying, she worked as a manicurist in a barbershop. And she fell in love. His name was Herbert Sheen and he was a good-looking medical student. "He could [play] a piano out of this world, sing . . . and dance beautifully," Zora remembered. "He noticed me, too, and I was carried away. For the first time since my mother's death, there was someone who felt really close and warm to me."

It was at Howard that Zora first began to publish her short stories. All her years of hardship, wandering, and adventure had improved her skills as a collector and teller of stories. Now she started to write her stories down. The literary club at Howard published a magazine of student writing. In the May 1921 issue, the magazine published a story by Zora Hurston. The story was called "John Redding Goes to Sea." John Redding is a man who wants to leave his small town to become a sailor so he can go to "where the sky touches the ground." In Zora's story, John Redding feels the same way that young Zora felt when she sat high up in the chinaberry tree looking out at the horizon.

Two years after "John Redding Goes to Sea" was published, Zora got a letter from a man named Charles S. Johnson. Johnson was the *editor* of a new magazine called *Opportunity: A Journal of Negro Life*. He was writing to all the black colleges in the country, looking for good young writers. He wanted to publish their stories and poems in his magazine.

Zora sent a story to Johnson. It was called "Drenched in Light." The main character in the story is a "small brown girl" named Isie. Just like John Redding and Zora herself, Isie wants to see what is over the horizon. Johnson published the story, and later on, he published another story by Zora called "Spunk."

Charles Johnson was impressed by Zora's

After almost 10 years of wandering, Hurston arrived in Baltimore, Maryland. There, in 1917, she enrolled in the Morgan Academy (pictured here) and took up her education once again.

stories. She was obviously a talented writer. He sent her a letter suggesting that she move to New York City, where many young, talented black writers and artists lived. Exciting things were happening there. New York City was another new horizon, and Zora wanted to move toward it. So, in her own words, "the first week of January, 1925, found me in New York with $1.50, no job, no friends, and a lot of hope."

Zora Neale Hurston arrived in Harlem, New York City, in 1925. Harlem was a center for black American culture, and there Hurston met many black artists, writers, performers, and political leaders. In Harlem, she also began to make a name for herself as a writer.

CHAPTER

3
Blackness

When Zora Hurston came to New York, she went to Harlem, a large African-American community in Manhattan. She had arrived at just the right moment. Harlem was a place of change and excitement in the 1920s. Many black soldiers had just returned to the United States from World War I. A lot of them decided to settle in the North, where there were new job opportunities. They brought their families with them. Over a million blacks left the South and moved north. Many of them settled in Harlem. As Harlem grew, strong black leaders emerged. These new leaders, such as Booker T. Washington and W. E. B. Du Bois, demanded political rights and equality for their people.

Black writers, painters, poets, dancers, musicians, and sculptors in Harlem were inspired by these exciting changes in black American society. People began talking about the *renaissance* that was happening in Harlem. (A renaissance is a time of great cultural and artistic activity in a society.)

Hurston began making her artistic mark on the Harlem Renaissance. In May 1925, she won two important prizes at the *Opportunity* magazine awards banquet. Hurston won second place for her short story "Spunk." She also received a second-place award for *Color Struck*, a play she had written. Zora Hurston was earning a reputation as a promising young writer. She was invited to parties and events, where she met other young black artists, such as the poets Langston Hughes and Countee Cullen. She also began to meet im-

Langston Hughes was one of the young black writers Hurston became friendly with in Harlem. Hughes loved to spend time with Hurston and listen to her colorful stories about life in the Deep South and her humorous observations about New York.

portant supporters of the arts, many of whom were wealthy white people.

Hurston was soon recognized as one of the liveliest personalities in the Harlem Renaissance. By now, Hurston was a mature, confident woman who knew a lot about the hardships of life. But she went about things in a joyous manner. She loved to dress up and go out to parties, to laugh and have a good time. She was known for telling funny stories in her deep, rich voice and southern accent. And there was also something mysterious about her. She usually lied about her age and often kept secrets about her past.

Some participants in the Harlem Renaissance did not approve of Hurston's actions. They thought that she was using her new reputation and her charm to get money and favors from important white people. Langston Hughes said that Zora "was always getting scholarships and things from wealthy white people, some of whom simply paid her just to sit around and represent the Negro race for them."

Other black people did not approve of Hurston's writing. More and more black writers were getting their work published. Many of them were thinking and talking about what black *literature* was and what they wanted it to be. A lot of African Americans believed that black writers should always write about racism and the struggle for *civil rights*. They believed that black writers had a responsibility to use their talents to help their fellow blacks who were suffering from racism and *discrimination*. They wanted Hurston to use her writing talents in this manner.

And many of Hurston's critics did not like the characters that she wrote about. The critics were concerned about the image of blacks in America. They believed that black writers should write about blacks who lived in cities and who were prosperous and well educated. They knew that whites believed many of the *stereotypes* about African Americans. According to these stereotypes, blacks were all poor, uneducated, and simpleminded. Hurston's critics wanted to destroy

A letter from Hurston to her friend Countee Cullen. In the letter, Hurston explains to Cullen why she does not want to write only about lynchings and other forms of racial injustice in America.

March 5, 1943

Dear Countee:

Thanks a million for your kind letter. I am always proud to have a word of praise from you because your friendship means a great deal to me.

Why don't I put something about lynchings in my books? As if all the world did not know about Negroes being lynched! My stand is this: either we must *do* something about it that the white man will understand and respect, or shut up. No whiner ever got any respect or relief. If some of us must die for human justice, then *let us die.* For my own part, this poor body of mine is not so precious that I would not be willing to give it up for a good cause.

You are right in assuming that I am indifferent to the pattern of things. I am. I have never liked stale phrases and bodyless courage. I have the nerve to walk my own way, however hard, in my search for reality, rather than climb upon the rattling wagon of wishful illusions.

Cheerio, good luck, and a happy encounter (with me) in the near future.

Sincerely,

Zora

these stereotypes. They disapproved of Hurston's characters, who were often uneducated and poor, and who spoke in a southern black *dialect*. They thought that these characters strengthened racial stereotypes, instead of weakening them.

Alice Walker, a more recent black writer, explained that "Zora Neale Hurston was very, very controversial. She was always doing things that everybody really wished she wouldn't do. That is, everybody except the really black, black people in the South who knew that she was being them. They weren't bothered. It was only when she carried their black, black, blackness up to the North and she showed it at high class dinner parties that people were outraged."

Hurston had her own ideas about writing. She knew how important it was to fight against racism and injustice. But she did not want to write only about that. She wanted to write about black life in the South, not just a certain part of black life, such as racism. She wanted to tell the kinds of stories she had heard back in Eatonville. She felt that these stories had important things to say about African-American culture. So Hurston kept on doing just what she wanted. She cared more about writing the stories from her heart than about pleasing people.

In the meantime, Hurston had not forgotten her education. In the fall of 1925, she enrolled at Barnard College, a women's college in New York. Although Hurston was the only black student at Barnard, she enjoyed being there. And it was at Barnard that she met Dr. Franz Boas, a man who would change her life forever.

Dr. Boas was a well-known cultural an-thropologist. (*Cultural anthropology* is the study of human culture.) Hurston took a class in cultural anthropology that Boas was teaching. She quickly became fascinated by the subject. Inspired by Boas, Hurston thought seriously about becoming an anthropologist. Boas liked Hurston's intelligence and enthusiasm. He encouraged her to study the cultural anthropology of African Americans. It was something she already knew a lot about.

46

Boas believed that one of the best ways for an anthropologist to understand a certain culture was to study the songs and stories of that culture. Hurston realized that she had been doing that all her life. In a way, she had always been an anthropologist of black American culture in the South. She had always felt that the stories and songs she had heard in Eatonville and in other places in the South were important. Boas was convinced that she was right. He suggested that she go on a field trip to the South as an anthropologist, to collect more of the songs and stories of her people.

To pay for her field trip, Dr. Boas got

Hurston poses on the running board of her Chevrolet, Sassy Susie. During the summer of 1927, Hurston drove her car around Florida, Louisiana, and Alabama, collecting the songs and stories of black Americans in the South.

Hurston some money from the Association for the Study of Negro Life and History. In February 1927, an excited Zora Hurston went south. She took a train to Jacksonville, Florida. There she bought a car, which she named Sassie Susie. Her plan was to drive around and talk to people, asking them to tell the stories and sing the songs they knew. Hurston would write down the stories and songs so they could be put in books and studied.

But after three months of driving around the Deep South, Hurston did not have many songs or stories down on paper. She had been away from the South for so long that many of the people she talked to thought she was an outsider. It was hard for Hurston to win their trust and get them to tell her their stories or sing their songs. Being an anthropologist was more difficult than she had imagined.

After three months, Hurston took some time off. She traveled to St. Augustine, Florida. There, in May 1927, she married Herbert Sheen, her sweetheart from her days at Howard University. Marriage seemed like a good idea until right after the wedding. Then it seemed like a bad idea. The newlyweds would not be together for long. Both Hurston and Sheen realized that their marriage was a mistake. Neither of them was ready for marriage, and they were divorced four years later.

Hurston returned to her anthropology work. One of her most interesting interviews was with a 90-year-old black man named Cudjo Lewis. Lewis had come to the United States from Africa on a slave ship when he was 19 years old. He told Hurston about his life in Africa and about what it was like to be a slave in Alabama. But aside from her interview with Cudjo Lewis, Hurston was still not having much success.

Not long after she talked to Cudjo Lewis, Hurston met one of her Harlem friends, the poet Langston Hughes. He had been touring the South and giving poetry readings. In August, Hurston and Hughes drove back to New York together in Sassy Suzie. The two young writers enjoyed each

Former slave Cudjo Lewis and two of his grandchildren. In July 1927, Hurston traveled to Mobile, Alabama, to interview Lewis about his memories of the days of slavery in the United States. Lewis was almost 90 years old.

other's company. They talked and laughed during the long, hot drive. (Hurston's husband had returned to Chicago, where he was studying to become a doctor.)

Although the ride back to New York with Hughes had been fun, Hurston was unhappy. She felt that she had failed as an anthropologist. As Hurston herself put it, she had not collected enough material to make a "jacket" for a "flea." But Dr. Boas gave her advice and encouragement. And then Langston Hughes introduced Hurston to one of his supporters, a wealthy white woman named Charlotte Mason. Mason supplied Hughes with money so that he could concentrate on his poetry without having to work at another job. She supported many young black artists in this manner. Soon she agreed to give Hurston money so she could continue her anthropology work. In December 1927, Zora Hurston went south again.

During the 1930s, Hurston traveled throughout the West Indies. This photograph of Hurston and her guide exploring a river in Jamaica was taken in 1935.

CHAPTER

4
Walking in
Storms

Zora Hurston's second anthropology field trip was much more successful than her first. It was also more exciting. Sometimes it was even dangerous. One of the places Hurston went to in order to collect songs and stories was a lumber camp in Polk County, Florida. A man who knew a lot of songs played guitar and sang in a tavern there. His name was Slim.

Every night, Hurston listened to Slim and wrote down his songs. But Slim's former girlfriend became jealous of Hurston. She said that Hurston had taken her man. One night she came to the tavern with a knife, looking for Hurston. Luckily, Hurston had made friends with the toughest woman in camp. Her name was Big Sweet. Big Sweet fought with the jealous woman while Hurston made a quick getaway in her car. She was so scared that she kept driving all night until she made it to New Orleans, Louisiana. After that, Hurston started to carry a gun on her trips.

In New Orleans, Hurston investigated a religion called hoodoo. It was an old religion that came to America with the black slaves from Africa. Many blacks in the Deep South practiced hoodoo. Hoodoo priests were called power doctors. They believed that hoodoo magic could be used to cause things to happen to people and to influence events.

Hurston tried to meet as many of the power doctors as she could. She wanted to learn all about hoodoo from them. She went through secret hoodoo ceremonies with the power doctors. One of them was called the Frizzly Rooster. Sometimes

Hurston was put into a *trance* and had strange dreams. She was made sister to a rattlesnake. The power doctors painted the symbol of lightning on her back and told her to walk in storms to get answers to her questions about life.

The last stop on Hurston's trip was the island of Nassau. Nassau is one of the Bahama Islands. Hurston had heard some of the folklore of the Bahamas while she was in Florida. She liked it so much that she took a boat over to Nassau to do some research. The people there made up songs for everything. One person told Hurston, "You do anything, we put you in sing." Hurston was careful not to do anything that might cause the islanders to make up a teasing song about her.

Hurston returned to Florida in October 1929. Her second anthropology field trip was a success. She had collected enough folklore to make a book. In 1930, Charlotte Mason gave Hurston money to support herself while she put her book together. She called it *Mules and Men.* Hurston moved into an apartment in Westfield, New Jersey, and got to work. Langston Hughes was also living in Westfield while he wrote his first novel.

Hurston and Hughes decided to write a play together. They wanted to write a comedy based on one of the stories Hurston had collected. They called their play *Mule Bone*. But before they could finish the play, Hurston and Hughes had an argument. Angrily, Hurston left Westfield and said she would finish the play herself. In January 1931, Hughes learned that *Mule Bone* was being performed in Cleveland. Zora Neale Hurston was listed as the play's only author. Hughes called Hurston and demanded some of the money from the play and credit as writer. Hurston refused. That was the end of the friendship between two of America's most important writers.

Hurston was upset about her falling-out with Langston Hughes. She regretted it all her life. So did Hughes. But she moved on to the next project, a Broadway show. She wanted to stage a black musical, with songs she had collected during her field trips. And she wanted the music to be performed just as it was in real life. Hurston borrowed enough money from Charlotte Mason to put on the show for one night. The show, called *The Great Day*, was performed at the John Golden Theater in New York on January 10, 1932. The audience loved it. Hurston made no money from *The Great Day*, but she felt that she had proved that audiences could enjoy African-American music in its true form.

Not long after the performance of *The Great Day*, Hurston returned to Eatonville. There she finished *Mules and Men*. But it would take her three years to find a publisher for *Mules and Men*. Soon Hurston was broke. And she was not the only one who had no money: the Great Depression was underway. This was a period of widespread unemployment and poverty in the United States. Hard times had come for Zora Hurston and millions of other Americans.

For Hurston, the hard times did not last. In 1933, she finished a short story called "The Gilded Six-Bits." A friend of Zora's sent it to a magazine

A scene from Hurston's Broadway musical, The Great Day. *The play was about black railroad workers, and it featured many of the songs Hurston had collected during her travels in the South.*

called *Story*. "The Gilded Six-Bits" was published. Bertram Lippincott, an important publisher in New York, read "The Gilded Six-Bits." He was impressed by it. Lippincott wrote to Hurston and asked if she had written a novel. If she had, he wanted to see it.

Hurston had an idea for a novel, called *Jonah's Gourd Vine*, but she had not started it yet. Now she moved to nearby Sanford, rented a cheap house, and started writing. Three months later, *Jonah's Gourd Vine* was in the mail to New York. Two weeks after that, Hurston received word that her novel would be published. She also received a check for $200. Although she had been kicked out of her house that morning, it was a great day for Zora Neale Hurston.

Jonah's Gourd Vine was published in 1934. The novel is about a black preacher who is a lot like Zora Hurston's father. The preacher lives in a town that resembles Eatonville. It is a tragic story in which the preacher destroys himself through violence and guilt. *Jonah's Gourd Vine* was very successful, and in 1935 *Mules and Men* was finally published. *Mules and Men* was also a success for Hurston. But again, some black readers did not like it.

Hurston's critics felt that *Mules and Men* showed black life as too peaceful and pleasant. They said that it was unrealistic because Hurston had left out the poverty, violence, and racism that southern blacks faced. But Hurston believed that black culture in America was something more than a response to white racism. She knew that it was important to write about the parts of black life that had nothing to do with white people or the problems of racism.

Zora Neale Hurston was now a successful and well-known writer, and she could afford to go on another trip. In 1935, she traveled to Jamaica, an island in the West Indies. In Jamaica, Hurston studied the Maroons. The Maroons were the descendants of slaves who were brought to Jamaica from Africa. They had fought their way to freedom in the hill country, where they formed their own community. Hurston stayed with the Maroons for months. The Maroons still lived a lot like their ancestors had lived in Africa before they were taken as slaves. They taught Hurston about herbal medicine, and she watched many of their religious ceremonies.

From Jamaica, Hurston traveled to Haiti, where she investigated the voodoo religion. Voodoo was similar to the hoodoo religion she had studied in Louisiana. In Haiti, Hurston witnessed secret voodoo ceremonies that she found "beautiful and terrifying." She also met someone who was said to be a zombie. Zombies, according to voodoo worshippers, are people who have returned from the dead. Hurston was told that the zombie she encountered had reappeared after being dead for 20 years. Being a good researcher, Zora took a photograph of the zombie.

Hurston tried to stay as busy as she could while she was in the West Indies. Back in 1934, she had fallen in love with a man she met in New York. Now she was trying to fall out of love.

Hurston took this photograph of a zombie in Haiti in 1936. According to the voodoo religion of Haiti, zombies are people who have returned from the dead.

Hurston was crazy about this man. "I did not just fall in love," she said about their affair. "I made a parachute jump." Unfortunately, the man wanted Hurston to give up her career as a writer and anthropologist. "He begged me to give up my career, marry him and live outside New York City," Hurston said. "I really wanted to do anything he wanted me to do, but that one thing I could not do."

Hurston had finally ended the relationship and sailed off to the West Indies. In Jamaica and Haiti, Hurston buried herself in her work to try and forget about the pain and sadness of the affair. But she could not forget. She was still in love, and she felt as if her heart were bleeding. Hurston decided to write another novel to help herself deal with her strong feelings. The novel she wrote was called *Their Eyes Were Watching God*. It became Hurston's most famous book.

Their Eyes Were Watching God is the story of a woman called Janie Crawford and her struggles to learn and grow. In the novel, Janie falls in love with a handsome man named Tea Cake Woods. Tea Cake dies tragically. But the experience of loving and losing Tea Cake helps Janie to learn things about herself and about life. Eventually, Janie finds wisdom, which allows her to be at peace with the world.

Their Eyes Were Watching God was published in 1937. Most readers felt that it was a beautiful story. Some people called it a masterpiece. But Hurston still could not satisfy her critics, who always seemed to find something wrong with her work. Even one of Hurston's old professors from Howard University criticized her for not writing stories about the problems that blacks faced in American society.

Hurston was angry, but she continued writing, determined not to become discouraged by the critics. Her next book, *Tell My Horse*, was about her adventures in Jamaica and Haiti. It was published in 1938, but it did not sell very well. The following year, she published another novel, called *Moses, Man of the Mountain*. Hurston hoped this novel would please her critics. The story compares the slavery of Jews in Egypt to the slavery of Africans in America. Although Hurston worked hard on this novel, it did not satisfy the critics, and Zora herself said that she was not satisfied with it either. "I don't think that I achieved all that I set out to do," she said to a friend.

In 1942, Hurston's *autobiography* was published. It was called *Dust Tracks on a Road*, and it turned out to be the most popular book she had written. But as usual, Hurston's black critics did not like it. They said that Hurston was just writing to please white readers. Hurt by the criticism, Hurston retreated to Florida. She bought a houseboat called the *Wanago*. For a while she led a peaceful life, boating up and down the Indian and Halifax rivers. She would fish in the daytime and write on the boat at night.

In May 1947, Hurston felt the urge to wander once again. This time she traveled to Honduras, a country in Central America. There, she settled down in a coastal town and wrote another

In 1942, Hurston, now 51 years old, published her autobiography, Dust Tracks on a Road. *It quickly became the most popular of all her books.*

novel, *Seraph on the Suwanee*. Published in 1948, *Seraph on the Suwanee* is about poor white people in Florida. Although the novel sold well, it is not considered to be one of Zora Hurston's best efforts. It would be the last novel she ever published.

Hurston was now 59 years old. She was working on a huge novel called "Herod the Great." In the spring of 1950, she ran out of money. Hurston did what she had always done in this situation: She went out and got a job. She

Hurston walks alone on a dusty road in the Central American country of Honduras in 1947. In Honduras, Hurston wrote her last published novel, Seraph on the Suwanee.

69

worked as a maid in Miami until 1951, when she earned $1,000 for an article she wrote for the *Saturday Evening Post* magazine. She used the money to rent a tiny cottage in the small town of Eau Gallie, Florida.

Hurston lived in her little cottage for six years. She fixed it up nicely, planted a garden, and got a little dog for company. And she continued working on "Herod the Great." Although she had little money and her health was failing, these were happy years for Hurston. "I am happier than I have been for at least ten years," she told an editor from her publishing company. Hurston was at peace with herself.

In 1955, Hurston's publishing company rejected "Herod the Great." They did not feel that it was good enough to be published. Hurston took this news calmly and went back to work on the book. A year later, her landlord sold Hurston's little cottage. Once again, Hurston became a nomad. She moved around a lot, working at odd jobs when she needed money. And she continued writing.

In 1959, Hurston had a stroke. By the end of the year, she was so ill that she had to move into a welfare home to be taken care of. In late January 1960, at the age of 69, Zora Neale Hurston died of a heart attack. She was buried in an unmarked grave. Thirteen years later, the writer Alice Walker traveled to Florida in search of Hurston's grave. She found the gravesite and placed a marker there. It said: A Genius of the South.

Alice Walker was just one of the many writers and scholars who recognized the true importance of Zora Neale Hurston. Today's black woman writers feel that they owe a lot to Hurston. Her work has inspired and guided them. Alice Walker has said that there is no book more important to her than *Their Eyes Were Watching God*. "Hurston," said another writer, Mary Helen Washington, "was determined to write about black life as it existed apart from racism, injustice, Jim Crow, where black people laughed, celebrated, loved, sorrowed and struggled, unconcerned about white people."

Zora Neale Hurston lived a hard life. She struggled to get an education, to have her work published, to overcome her critics, and even to keep a roof over her head. She struggled to survive racism and poverty. But she lived life to the fullest. And like Janie in *Their Eyes Were Watching God*, she came to understand life deeply. In *Dust Tracks on a Road*, Zora Neale Hurston wrote: "I feel that I have lived. I have had the joy and pain of strong friendships. I have served and been served. I have made enemies of which I am not ashamed. I have been faithless, and then I have been faithful . . . until the blood ran down into my shoes. I have loved unselfishly . . . and I have hated with all the power of my soul. . . . I have touched the four corners of the horizon, for from hard searching it seems to me that tears and laughter, love and hate, make up the sum of life."

72

Further Reading

Other biographies of Zora Neale Hurston

Lyons, Mary. *Sorrow's Kitchen*. New York: Scribners, 1990.

Zora is My Name! Beverly Hills, CA: PBS Home Video, 1990. Video recording.

Related Works

Walker, Alice. *Langston Hughes, American Poet*. New York: Harper Junior Books, 1974.

Alice Walker interview with Kay Bonetti. Columbia, MO: American Audio Prose Library, 1981. Sound recording.

Chronology

1932 Produces *The Great Day* in New York City

1934 *Jonah's Gourd Vine* is published

1935 *Mules and Men* is published

1936 Hurston takes anthropology field trip to Jamaica and Haiti

1937 *Their Eyes Were Watching God* is published

1939 *Moses, Man of the Mountain* is published

1942 *Dust Tracks on a Road* is published

1947 Hurston travels to Honduras

1948 *Seraph on the Suwanee* is published

1955 Publishers reject "Herod the Great"

1959 Hurston suffers a stroke; enters welfare home

1960 Zora Neale Hurston dies in Fort Pierce, Florida, on January 28

Glossary

atlas   a book of maps

autobiography   the story of a person's life written or told by that person

civil rights   the personal and property rights of an individual recognized by a government and its laws and constitution

cultural anthropology   the study of human culture

dialect   a variety of a language that is spoken by a particular group or spoken in a certain part of a country

discrimination   the unfair treatment of a certain group of people; prejudice

editor   one who prepares a piece of writing for publication

folklore   traditions such as customs, legends, songs, or art forms that are part of a group's culture

folktale   a story circulated orally among a people, handed down from one generation to the next

Jim Crow laws   laws enforcing segregation and discrimination against black Americans and named after a character from minstrel shows during the 19th century

literature   written works that have lasting value and interest

mythology   a collection of stories about the gods and legendary heroes of a particular people

Norse   of or relating to ancient Scandinavia, its people, or their language

operetta   a short comic opera that includes songs and dancing

racism   a belief that one's own race is superior

renaissance   a period of great artistic revival and cultural activity in a society

segregation   the policy of keeping people of different races separate, as in schools, housing, and industry

stereotype   a fixed idea about a person or group that is untrue or incomplete and overlooks individual characteristics

trance   a mental condition resembling sleep that can be caused by being hypnotized

Index

Roz Calvert attended the Center for Creative Arts at West Virginia University and currently lives in New York City. She is the author of a mystery novel, *Bluff*, and two feature-length screenplays. Her poetry has appeared in *Sinister Wisdom* and *Naming the Waves Anthology*.

Picture Credits

Courtesy of the Jane Belo Estate: p. 52; The Bettmann Archive: pp. 18–19, 68–69; The Countee Cullen Papers, the Amistad Research Center, Tulane University, New Orleans, Louisiana: p. 44; Courtesy of the Department of Rare Books and Manuscripts, University of Florida Library, Gainesville: p.29, 58–59, 67; Courtesy of Dr. West and the Mugar Memorial Library, Boston University: p. 47; Florida State Archives, Tallahassee: pp. 12–13, 15; Erik Overbey Collection, University of Southern Alabama, Mobile: p. 50; Photo from *Tell My Horse* by Zora Neale Hurston. Copyright 1938 by Zora Neale Hurston. Copyright renewed 1966 by Joel Hurston and John C. Hurston. Reprinted by permission of HarperCollins Publishers: p. 63; Courtesy of Robert Hemenway: p. 26; Courtesy of Sheen Educational Foundation Library and the University of Florida Library, Gainesville: p. 22; Courtesy of Special Collections Library, Morgan State University, Baltimore, MD: p. 36; UPI/Bettmann: p. 38; Courtesy of the Carl Van Vechten Estate, Joseph Solomon, Executor. Print from the Schomburg Center for Research in Black Culture, The New York Public Library, Astor, Lenox, and Tilden Foundations: frontis, pp. 6, 41